W9-BXE-204

I'm Tougher Than Asthma!

Alden R. Carter and Siri M. Carter

Photographs by Dan Young

Albert Whitman & Company • Morton Grove, Illinois

For the Sutterers and the O'Brien-Nelsons.
S.M.C. and A.R.C.

For Nancy, Dustin, Janet, Trudy, and Paul. D.M.Y.

Thanks to all who helped with *I'm Tougher Than Asthma!* particularly
Gerald Bucholtz, M.D., Marliss Trudeau, Jim Cain, Karen Katzenberger,
Jack Bittrich, Graham Olson, John Campbell, M.D., Kathy Campbell,
Barb Bartkowiak, Lisa Weister, Jim Fredrick, Peg Pesicka, Mary Rehlinger,
Judy and Michel Roy, Mary Hofer, Sarah Blanchard, Mary McClung, and
all Siri's classmates and teammates. Our families and our editor,
Abby Levine, have our special gratitude.

About the Authors and Photographer

Siri M. Carter attends Washington Elementary School
in Marshfield, Wisconsin. She particularly enjoys toads,
singing, baseball, and the piano. This is her first book.
Besides being Siri's dad, **Alden R. Carter** is the author of seven novels
and twenty nonfiction books for children and young adults. In 1994, his
novel *Up Country* was named one of the Best 100 Books for Young Adults
of the Last 25 Years by the American Library Association.

Dan Young is the award-winning photojournalist of the *Marshfield
News Herald.* His work has appeared in the *Washington Post,* the *Milwaukee
Journal, Current Science,* and numerous other newspapers and magazines,
as well as internationally through the Associated Press. In 1995, he was
awarded Best of Show by the Wisconsin News Photographers Association.
This is his first book.

Text copyright © 1996 by Alden R. Carter and Siri M. Carter.
Photographs copyright ©1996 by Dan Young.
Published in 1996 by Albert Whitman & Company,
6340 Oakton Street, Morton Grove, Illinois 60053-2723.
Published simultaneously in Canada
by General Publishing, Limited, Toronto.
Printed in the United States of America.
10 9 8 7 6 5 4 3 2 1
Design by Karen A.Yops.

Model of human body, p. 9: Courtesy Sargent Welch; dust mite, p. 12: Photo ©
Andrew Syred/Science Photo Library/Photo Researchers; photo of Theodore
Roosevelt, p. 26: Theodore Roosevelt Collection, Harvard College Library.

Library of Congress Cataloging-in-Publication Data

Carter, Alden R.
I'm tougher than asthma! / written by Alden Carter and Siri M.
Carter; photographs by Dan Young.
p. cm.
Includes bibliographical references.
Summary: A young girl describes what it is like to live with
asthma, how this condition affects the body, some of the things
that trigger an attack, and what can be done to avoid
problems.
ISBN 0-8075-3474-9
1. Asthma—Juvenile literature. [1. Asthma.] I. Carter, Siri M.
II. Young, Dan, photographer, ill. III. Title.
RC591.C384 1996   95-32077
616.2'38—dc20   CIP
                                   AC

A Note for Parents of Children with Asthma

What I remember most vividly about Siri's first asthma attack was how her panting and wheezing seemed to shake the bed. I lay beside her as she tried to sleep, and I tried to imagine why her cold had taken such a terrible turn. The thought that she was having an asthma attack never entered my head.

When my husband, Alden, returned from a speaking engagement late that evening, he quickly became as frightened and confused as I was. As soon as a friend arrived to stay with our sleeping son, we left for the hospital.

Neither the admitting physician nor the specialist we saw the next day had any doubt that Siri was suffering from asthma. We were stunned. No one in either of our families had ever been troubled with asthma, but here was our little girl fighting a condition we knew almost nothing about. We would learn a great deal about it in the next five years as we worked with Siri to manage her asthma.

Our son, Brian, four years older than Siri, had always been a very attentive brother. It was hard for him when we had to give our aging cat to a friend, but he never blamed Siri. Instead, he learned to help her with her medication and to explain her asthma to her in ways that escaped her parents.

Siri gained confidence as she understood more about her asthma and took a hand in its management. She learned that with medication she could be as active as any of her playmates almost all the time. She also learned that every so often her asthma would make her feel awful, but that she would endure and feel "great" again.

This is Siri's book. Alden helped with the words and Dan shot the pictures, but Siri has been the one to live the story—a story that she told us she wanted to share with some other kids who are tougher than asthma but who may not know it just yet.

Carol S. Carter

Hi, I'm Siri. I like toads,

and listening to stories in Mrs. Trudeau's class,

and playing with my friends.

And, oh yeah, I've got asthma, which I don't like because sometimes it gets in the way of having fun. Asthma can make it hard for me to breathe. So four times a day, I take medicine to help my lungs.

My asthma started when I was three and had a real bad cold. I don't remember much except that it felt like this great big animal—a tiger, maybe—was sitting on my chest. I coughed a lot, and my lungs made a whistling, wheezing sound.

I was scared when Mom and Dad took me to the emergency room, but the people there gave me medicine that helped me breathe. I spent the night in the hospital, and the next day I met Dr. Bucholtz. He checked me over and told Mom, Dad, and me about asthma.

I learned this is what lungs look like. When I'm well, these little breathing tubes, called airways, are nice and open. But when my asthma gets bad, they get narrow and clog up with yucky, gooey stuff called mucus. The medicine I take every day helps keep the airways open and healthy.

Usually, it's a cold that makes my asthma really bad. But sometimes it's my allergies. People can be allergic to all sorts of stuff—weeds, mold, bug bites, even milk and peanut butter! Most people just get a rash, or cough and sneeze a little from their allergies, but people with asthma can get really sick.

Like my friend Dusty, I had allergy tests when I first got asthma. A nurse is testing a bunch of things on little scratches she's made on his back. If he's allergic to something, he'll get a bump like a mosquito bite.

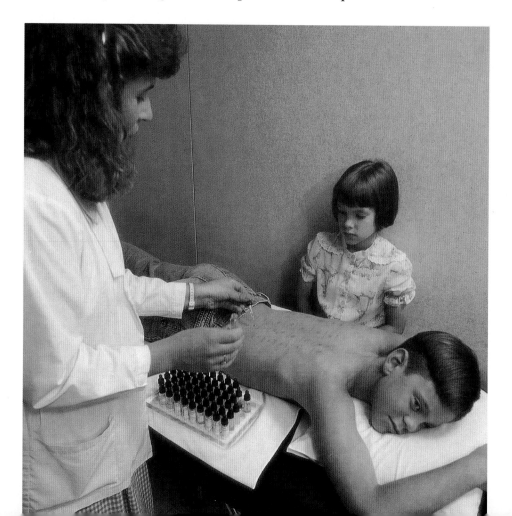

When I had my tests, we found out that I was real allergic to animal dander. That's the flaking skin beneath fur. I can't have a dog or cat of my own because they'd leave dander around the house, but I can take my pal Dickens for a walk. Besides dander, I'm allergic to . . . Are you ready for this?

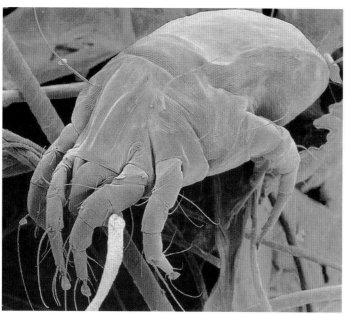

A dust mite (magnified) crawling among hair and other fibers in household dust.

House dust mites! Pretty gross, huh? They're too small to see, but every house has them in the dust, especially in carpeting, pillows, and mattresses. They like damp places, so we keep the air in our house dry. We have a special filter in our furnace and a fancy vacuum cleaner to catch as much dust as we can. My brother, Brian, does the vacuuming every Saturday—if my mom or dad can catch him before he gets out of the house.

Mom bought big plastic envelopes to cover my pillow and mattress to keep the mites away from me when I'm sleeping. Once a week we wash my blankets and sheets in really hot water to kill any mites. I can't sleep with stuffed animals except my favorite bunny, which we keep extra clean.

I'm lucky not to be allergic to flower or weed pollen like lots of people are. I spend so much time outdoors that Mom calls me "Nature Girl."

Some real smelly stuff can give me trouble with my asthma, too. I stay away from hair spray, bleach, strong perfume, and especially cigarette smoke. When we had our rugs shampooed, we all slept outside in the camper. Good deal!

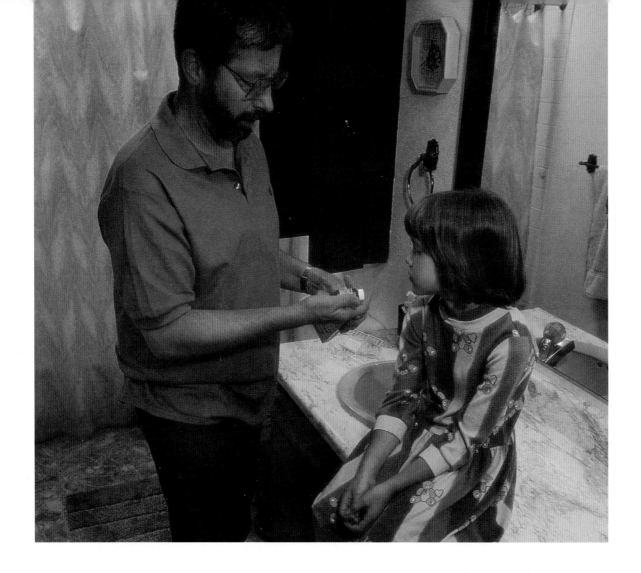

Most of the time, I feel great. But every once in a while I get a cold or my allergies get a lot worse. Then the airways in my lungs get narrow and full of mucus, and I start panting, wheezing, and coughing. This is called an asthma attack, and it's scary! But I practice being calm and brave while I'm waiting for the medicine that will help stop the attack.

When my asthma's bad, Mom or Dad will come in during the night to give me extra medicine. They use a machine called a nebulizer to turn some liquid medicine into a mist that I can breathe without waking up.

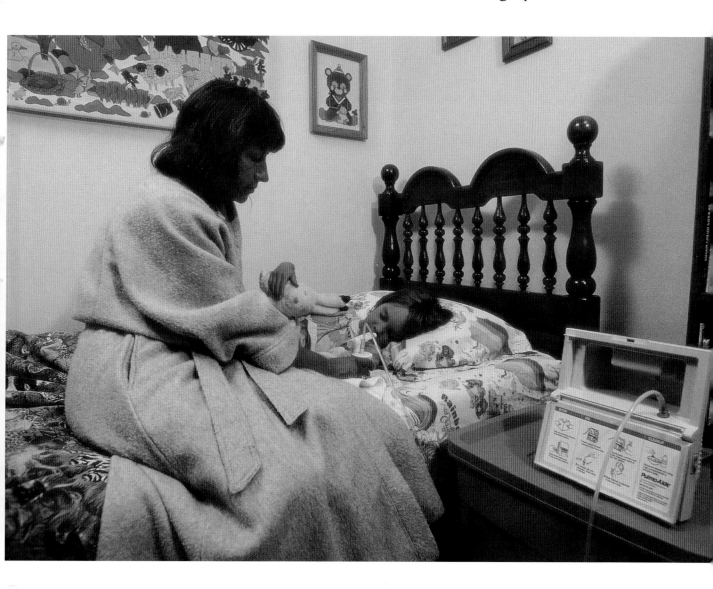

Sometimes I have to stay home for a couple of days before I'm feeling good again. But I have fun coloring, reading, or doing puzzles with my bunny.

And pretty soon, I'm back with my friends.

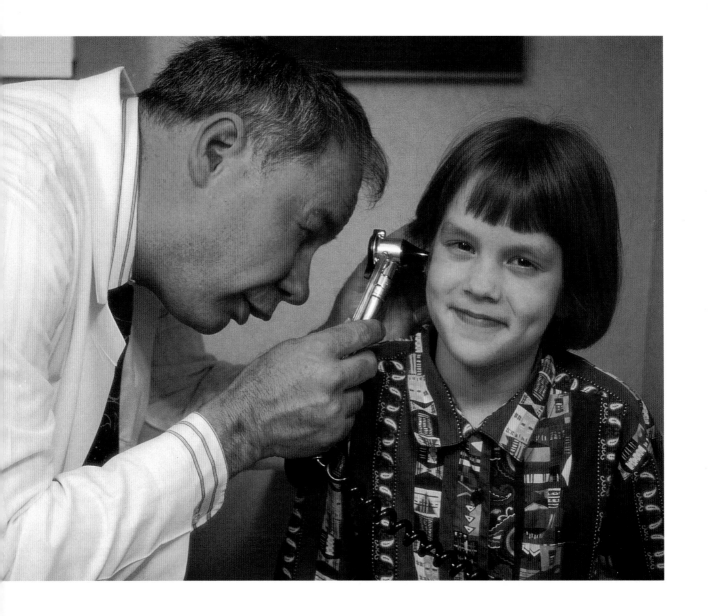

Every few months, Dr. Bucholtz gives me a checkup. He says that when I get bigger, my asthma may get better. I may always have some asthma, but that's okay since I'm learning how to handle it.

I stay in good shape so I can fight my asthma. I'm never, ever going to smoke or do anything dumb that could hurt my lungs.

I'm starting to take my asthma medicine on my own, and I'm learning to use a peak flow meter. It measures how well my lungs are working and tells when I need more medicine.

I'm also learning breathing exercises to help me if I feel an attack coming.

And so I can understand my asthma better, I'm keeping a diary with pictures of some of the things that bother me. This is Horrid, the House Dust Mite.

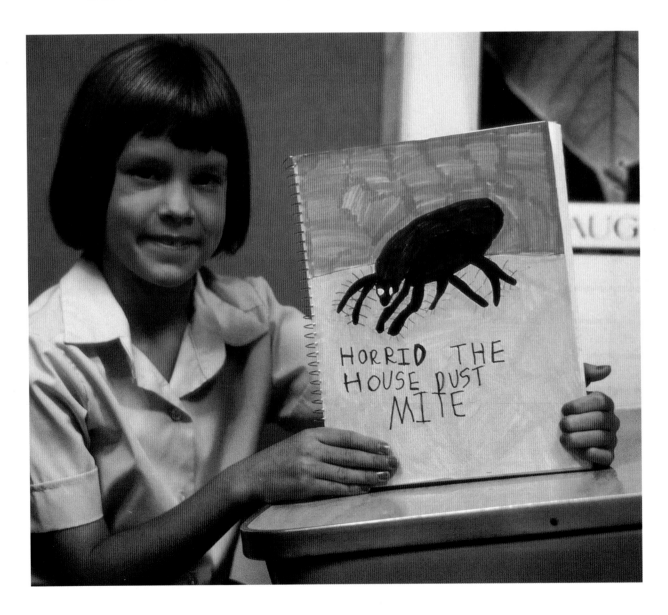

This summer I went to singing camp. When I grow up, I want to be a singer and an actress. You need good lungs for that, and mine can be as good as anyone's if I take care of them.

My dad says a lot of famous people have fought asthma: Jackie Joyner-Kersee, the Olympic runner; Robert Joffrey, the famous dance master; and Teddy Roosevelt, the president who looked like a walrus. They didn't let asthma slow them down, and I'm not going to let it slow me down.

Because I'm tougher than asthma!

More About Asthma

1. What is asthma?

Asthma is a lung disorder characterized by recurrent attacks of breathing difficulty. Attacks may last for minutes or for days. Over two thousand years ago, Greek physicians described and treated the condition, giving it the name *asthma* from the Greek verb meaning "to pant."

Asthma can be found in every climate and racial group. Today, more than twelve million people in the United States have been diagnosed with asthma. It is one of the nation's fastest-growing health problems. About 7 percent of children experience some asthma, and it is the leading cause of school absenteeism and hospitalization for children.

2. What causes asthma?

Medical research has yet to explain the causes of asthma completely. Heredity plays a role, making some people predisposed. However, an outside factor seems necessary to activate the asthma. Childhood culprits include premature birth, bronchial infections, allergies to food and pollen, and eczema. Fifty to 70 percent of childhood asthma sufferers experience their first attack by the age of three.

3. Why is asthma increasing?

Scientists have suggested a variety of causes for the increased incidence of asthma in industrialized nations. Auto and industrial emissions produce a complex mix of pollutants in the air. People are spending more time in tightly insulated buildings without adequate ventilation. Carpeting, plastics, and construction materials introduced in recent years may contain chemicals that produce asthmatic reactions.

4. What triggers an asthma attack?

Allergens and irritants trigger the majority of asthma attacks. Common airborne allergens include pollen, the feces of dust mites, mold spores, and animal dander and saliva. Certain foods, such as milk, fish, peanut butter, nuts, eggs, and chocolate, can be allergens. Aspirin, nonsteroidal anti-inflammatories such as ibuprofen, and sulfite preservatives in food and beverages can also cause asthmatic reactions.

Common irritants include cigarette and fireplace smoke, chemical and paint fumes, and hair sprays and perfumes. Other triggers include colds, flu, and bronchial infections; strenuous exercise; and cold air or rapid changes in the weather.

Skin and blood tests can detect many allergies. But just as most allergy sufferers do not have asthma, many people with asthma do not have allergies. Determining what triggers their asthma is often a matter of trial and error.

5. What happens during an asthma attack?

When the airways in an asthma sufferer's lungs are irritated, their linings become inflamed and swollen and the muscles around the airways contract. Glands along the linings begin producing mucus that clogs the already constricted airways. The difficulty of moving air through the narrowed airways produces the wheezing, panting, and coughing that are typical in an attack.

6. How can an asthma attack be predicted?

Symptoms of a coming attack include a feeling of tightness in the chest, coughing, restlessness while trying to fall asleep, breathlessness, and wheezing. Symptoms of serious attacks include flared nostrils, bluish lips, rapid breathing, an accelerated pulse rate, more pronounced wheezing, and difficulty in speaking more than a few words between breaths. The asthma sufferer may also sit slumped forward with shoulders raised.

For moderate or severe cases of asthma, doctors often recommend the use of a peak flow meter, a simple device that measures the outflow of air from the lungs. The peak flow is established by taking a series of readings when the patient is well. A subsequent reading substantially below that peak flow can indicate an approaching asthma attack and the need for additional medication.

7. What medications are available?

Many asthma sufferers take anti-inflammatories on a daily schedule to increase their lungs' resistance to inflammation. Allergy shots may also help.

During an asthma attack, medication can keep the airways open by reducing inflammation, relaxing tight muscles, and curtailing the production of mucus. Over-the-counter cold medications may help if the asthma attack is triggered by a cold or sinus infection, but should be taken only with a doctor's advice. Usually, an attack can be treated at home, but severe instances may require a visit to the emergency room or hospitalization.

8. What arrangements should I make with my child's school?

Discuss your child's condition and medical treatment with school personnel. If medication is necessary during the school day, work out a schedule. Since many schools require secure storage of medicines, your child may have to go to the nurse's or the principal's office for medication. Very young children will need assistance in using an inhaler, but by age eight or nine, most children require minimal supervision. Provide the school with written instructions to follow in an emergency.

Your child may have to avoid the class hamster, gerbil, or other furry mascot. If there is carpeting in the classroom, suggest treating it with an insecticide to kill dust mites. If classmates show curiosity about your child's asthma, visit the classroom so that together you and your child can explain.

9. How can I control airborne allergens in my home?

A number of products can help control airborne allergens. These include furnace filters, air purifiers, air conditioners, vacuum cleaners, foam pillows, plastic cases for mattresses and pillows, insecticides to kill dust mites, and fungicides to eliminate mold. It may be necessary to replace carpeting—particularly in bedrooms—with tile, linoleum, or wood flooring. Since animal dander and saliva are among the most common allergens, you will probably have to find another home for your pet. Removing house plants will eliminate indoor sources of pollen.

10. What can I do about chemical irritants?

Avoid unnecessary perfumes, cosmetics, and sprays. Mild household cleaners and "elbow grease" are preferable to harsher cleaners. If painting, renovating, or heavy cleaning is being done in the home, the asthma sufferer should stay away until the work is done and the house thoroughly ventilated. If you smoke, quit for your child's and your own good health.

11. Can children with asthma exercise and play sports?

Yes! Many famous athletes have overcome asthma with their doctors' help. Exercise can improve lung capacity, and children with asthma should be encouraged to participate in sports and playground activities. Taking asthma medication before a game or a race and warming up gradually will diminish the chance that strenuous exercise will bring on an attack.

12. What role do emotions play in asthma?

Crying, anger, frustration, and even laughter can cause breathing irregularities for asthma sufferers. People with asthma should learn to deal with stressful situations calmly and reasonably—a healthy goal for people without asthma as well. Asthma is not a symptom of emotional illness, as was once believed.

13. How can I help my child deal with asthma?

Encourage your child to participate in normal activities and to take control of his or her asthma. As soon as possible, children should learn to take daily medication and to use a peak flow meter, if they have one. It is also important for children to learn how to avoid their asthma triggers.

Even very young children can learn breathing exercises that will ease or avert an asthma attack. If an attack does occur, remain calm. In this way, you will reassure your child of his or her ability to endure and recover.

14. Do children outgrow asthma?

A majority of children find that their asthma improves during adolescence as their lungs mature and become more resistant to allergic inflammation. Many adolescents see their symptoms disappear altogether. Later in life, however, some outside factor may reactivate their asthma. Still, nearly everyone with asthma can live a full and productive life by learning the facts about asthma and following medical advice.

RESOURCES

The following organizations offer free or modestly priced books, pamphlets, videotapes, and educational programs.

Asthma & Allergy Foundation of America (AAFA)
1125 15th St. NW, Suite 502
Washington, D.C. 20005-2707
Phone: 202-466-7643;
800-7-ASTHMA
Fax: 202-466-8940

Allergy & Asthma Network/Mothers of Asthmatics (AAN/MA)
3554 Chain Bridge Rd., Suite 200
Fairfax, VA 22030-2709
Phone: 800-878-4403
Fax: 703-352-4354

American Lung Association (ALA)
1740 Broadway
New York, N.Y. 10019-4374
Phone: 212-315-8700
Fax: 212-265-5642

National Jewish Center for Immunology & Respiratory Medicine
1400 Jackson St.
Denver, CO 80206-2762
Phone: 303-388-4161
Lung Line: 800-222-LUNG

Books

Many wonderful books have been published on asthma and allergies. These are but a few of the best.

Haas, Francois, and Sheila Sperber Haas. *The Essential Asthma Book.* New York: Ballantine/Ivy, 1988.

Hannaway, Paul J., M.D. *The Asthma Self-Help Book: How to Live a Normal Life in Spite of Your Condition.* Rocklin, CA: Prima Publishing, 1991.

Harrington, Geri. *The Asthma Self-Care Book: How to Take Control of Your Asthma.* New York: HarperCollins, 1992.

Kerby, Mona. *Asthma.* New York: Franklin Watts, 1989.

Plaut, Thomas F., M.D. *Children with Asthma: A Manual for Parents.* Amherst, MA: Pedipress, 1988.

_____. *One-Minute Asthma.* Amherst, MA: Pedipress, 1991.